ALTERNATOR BOOKS™

THE MOON FILES

LIVING ON THE MOON

Diane Lindsey Reeves

Lerner Publications ◆ Minneapolis

Lerner Publications Company
An imprint of Lerner Publishing Group, Inc.
241 First Avenue North
Minneapolis, MN 55401 USA

For reading levels and more information, look up this title at www.lernerbooks.com.

Main body text set in Aptifer Sans LT Pro.
Typeface provided by Linotype.

Library of Congress Cataloging-in-Publication Data

Names: Reeves, Diane Lindsey, 1959–author.
Title: Living on the moon / Diane Lindsey Reeves.
Description: Minneapolis, MN : Lerner Publications, [2025] | Series: Alternator books. The moon files | Includes bibliographical references and index. | Audience: Ages 8–12 | Audience: Grades 4–6 | Summary: "Will humans one day live on the moon? Readers will love learning about what must happen in order for humans to live on the moon, including up-to-date information on this exciting topic"—Provided by publisher.
Identifiers: LCCN 2023048803 (print) | LCCN 2023048804 (ebook) | ISBN 9798765625583 (library binding) | ISBN 9798765629819 (paperback) | ISBN 9798765637883 (epub)
Subjects: LCSH: Space biology—Juvenile literature. | Moon—Juvenile literature. | Moon—Exploration—Juvenile literature.
Classification: LCC QB582 .R533 2025 (print) | LCC QB582 (ebook) | DDC 629.45/4—dc23/eng/20231103

LC record available at https://lccn.loc.gov/2023048803
LC ebook record available at https://lccn.loc.gov/2023048804

Manufactured in the United States of America
1 – CG – 7/15/24

Note to Readers: Images showing people living on the moon come from the imaginations of artists. They reflect ideas about how things might someday be.

TABLE OF CONTENTS

This art shows what it could look like to have a base camp on the moon.

INTRODUCTION

HOME SWEET MOON

Living on the moon sounds like something out of a movie. Where would you sleep? What would you eat? Could you play soccer in a spacesuit?

Scientists are busy working on answers to questions such as these and many more. After all, living on the moon has never happened before!

When people move from one place to another, they also may have many questions. But everywhere on Earth, there is oxygen to breathe. And most places have water to drink and the materials needed to build homes and towns.

Living on the moon takes things to a whole new level. What do humans need to make it work? How close are international space agencies and private companies to making it happen? Let's explore some answers.

The moon is 238,855 miles (384,400 km) from Earth.

CHAPTER 1

THE MOON UP CLOSE

Anaxagoras' discovery about the moon allowed him to explain lunar phases and eclipses.

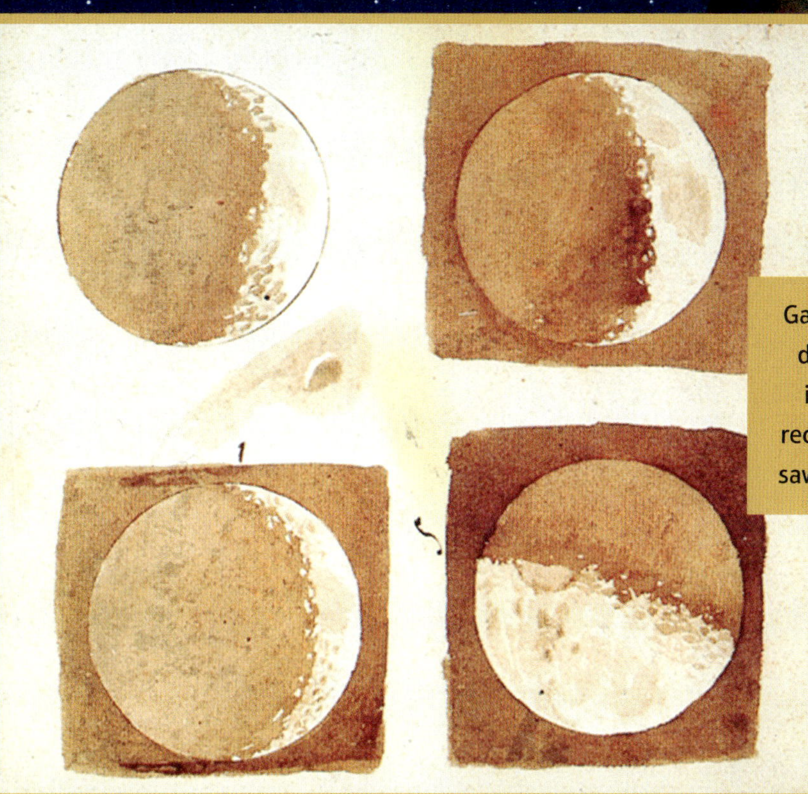

Galileo Galilei drew these images to record how he saw the moon.

People have been curious about the moon for thousands of years. Ancient humans could see it in the night sky. They just didn't know what it was or how it worked.

Perhaps the first discovery about the moon was made around 450 BCE by an ancient Greek philosopher named Anaxagoras. He realized that the moon does not shine with its own light. Its light is reflected from the sun.

Later, in 1609, an Italian astronomer named Galileo Galilei made his own telescope. He used it to study the sky and made a surprising observation. At the time, everyone thought the moon was smooth. Galileo saw that the moon was more like Earth. It had mountains, craters, and other features.

NASA launched its first space satellite, Pioneer 1, in 1958.

Space Race

It wasn't until the 1900s that humans began to study the moon up close. First it was with space probes. The Soviet Union (USSR) was a nation in eastern Europe and Asia until it split into Russia and fourteen other countries in 1991. In 1959 the Soviet Union sent Luna 2 to the moon. It was the very first space probe to the moon.

At the time, the United States was competing with the Soviets to be the first to make discoveries in space. The two countries continued to send space probes to the moon for several years. The space race was on! At first the Soviets were ahead.

Then the National Aeronautics and Space Agency (NASA) launched an exciting new space program called Apollo in 1961. Its goal was to land the first humans on the moon.

The Apollo missions included 11 spaceflights. Four flights tested equipment. Six flights landed people on the moon. One flight, Apollo 13, had to be aborted. After an explosion on Apollo 13, the crew circled the moon but did not land on it. But they landed safely back on Earth.

The US was first to land humans on the moon.

Apollo 17 astronaut Harrison Schmitt collects lunar rock samples.

Men on the Moon

Apollo 11 made history in 1969 when it landed the first humans on the moon. Astronaut Neil Armstrong was the first person to walk on it.

Apollo 17 was the last crewed spaceship to land on the moon. That was in 1972. A total of 12 people have walked on the moon so far. But that is about to change.

Left to right: Neil Armstrong, Michael Collins, and Buzz Aldrin were the first astronauts to land on the moon.

NASA astronaut Jasmin Moghbeli works on a science experiment while aboard the International Space Station.

CHAPTER 2

ALL ABOARD THE ISS

The International Space Station (ISS) is helping us figure out how to live outside of Earth's atmosphere. The ISS is where astronauts from around the world learn to live in space. Several countries worked together to build it starting in 1998. People could live on it since 2000, when astronauts started staying there on months-long missions.

The space station is in orbit about 250 miles (402 km) above Earth. It circles Earth every 90 minutes at a speed of 5 miles (8 km) per second. Every day, it travels through 16 sunrises and sunsets.

The space station has six bedrooms and two bathrooms. There is a gym for astronauts to use for daily workouts. Over 271 people from 21 different countries have visited the space station. There are usually three to six people onboard. Their missions on the ISS tend to last about six months.

The International Space Station is in orbit 248 miles (400 km) above Earth.

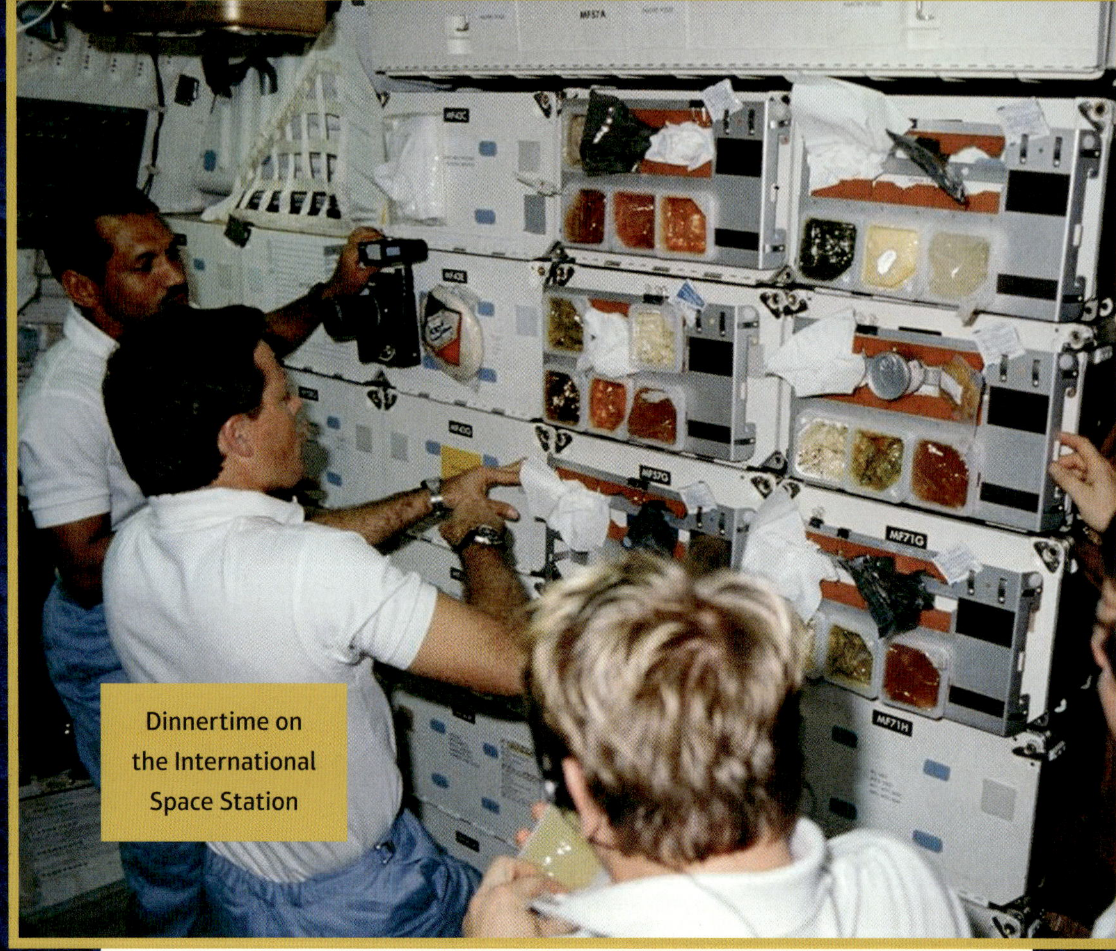

Dinnertime on the International Space Station

Space Munchies

In space, astronauts eat a mix of fresh and freeze-dried foods. The big rule for space food is no crumbs! In zero gravity, crumbs can float all over and might mess up important equipment. Some astronauts say that peanut butter is a nearly perfect space food.

Astronauts on the ISS stay busy by doing experiments. Every once in a while, they go outside for spacewalks. For fun, they work on hobbies, listen to music, or watch movies.

Survival of the Fittest

Getting humans ready to live on the moon is one of the space station's most important jobs.

Experiments on the ISS help scientists learn how humans can thrive in a microgravity environment. Scientists have learned how to grow food in space. They have also made improvements in how to handle human waste and hygiene.

Astronauts in space must exercise 2.5 hours per day to protect their bones and muscles from the effects of zero gravity.

Earth's magnetic field protects us from the sun's most harmful radiation.

One of the biggest challenges to living in space is radiation exposure. Earth's magnetic field helps shield everything living on our planet from radiation. But space does not have a magnetic field—and neither do the moon or Mars. Cosmic radiation damages human cells and causes cancer. It can even kill people. Scientists have to solve this problem before people can live on the moon.

Scientists are injecting tardigrade DNA into human cells. When exposed to radiation, these altered cells suffer 80 percent less damage than human cells.

LESSONS FROM NATURE

Scientists are looking to nature to solve the radiation problem. One study includes a tiny creature called a tardigrade, or water bear. It is only 0.2 inches (0.5 cm) long, and it can survive in extreme conditions, including space.

Tardigrades can go without food or water for decades and survive extreme temperatures.

Producing water in space is essential for survival. ISS astronauts are experimenting with different methods.

CHAPTER 3

STAYING ALIVE IN SPACE

Living on the moon will be very different from living on Earth. For starters, there is no oxygen in the moon's atmosphere. Humans need oxygen to live. Without it, the human brain starts to die within four to six minutes.

So far, astronauts on the moon have solved this problem by bringing oxygen with them. Scientists now look to two other possible solutions. One is water. The other is rocks.

You can pull oxygen out of water with a process called electrolysis. Astronauts aboard the ISS use electricity from solar panels to split water into hydrogen and oxygen gases. This is how they breathe inside the space station.

Scientists recently discovered water on the moon. This is good news. If water is already there, astronauts don't need to bring it. Scientists are racing to figure out how to tap into this resource. India's Chandrayaan-3 lunar module started exploring the moon's south pole in August 2023. It is searching for water ice.

Chandrayaan 3 was built by the Indian Space Research Organisation to land on the moon's south pole.

NASA looks to find ways to extract oxygen from lunar rocks.

A Breath of Fresh Rocks

Another source of oxygen on the moon is rocks. Oxygen can combine with other elements to form oxides. In rocks, they combine with metals to form a solid oxide. The rocky surface of the moon is rich in oxygen. NASA says moon rocks contain enough oxygen to support 8 billion people for 100,000 years.

But there is a problem. The oxygen is not in the gaseous state we need to breathe it. Many studies are underway to solve this problem.

Extracting oxygen from space rocks would not only provide oxygen for people to breathe. It could also provide an important ingredient for fuel. This would allow humans to stay longer on the moon and travel even farther into space.

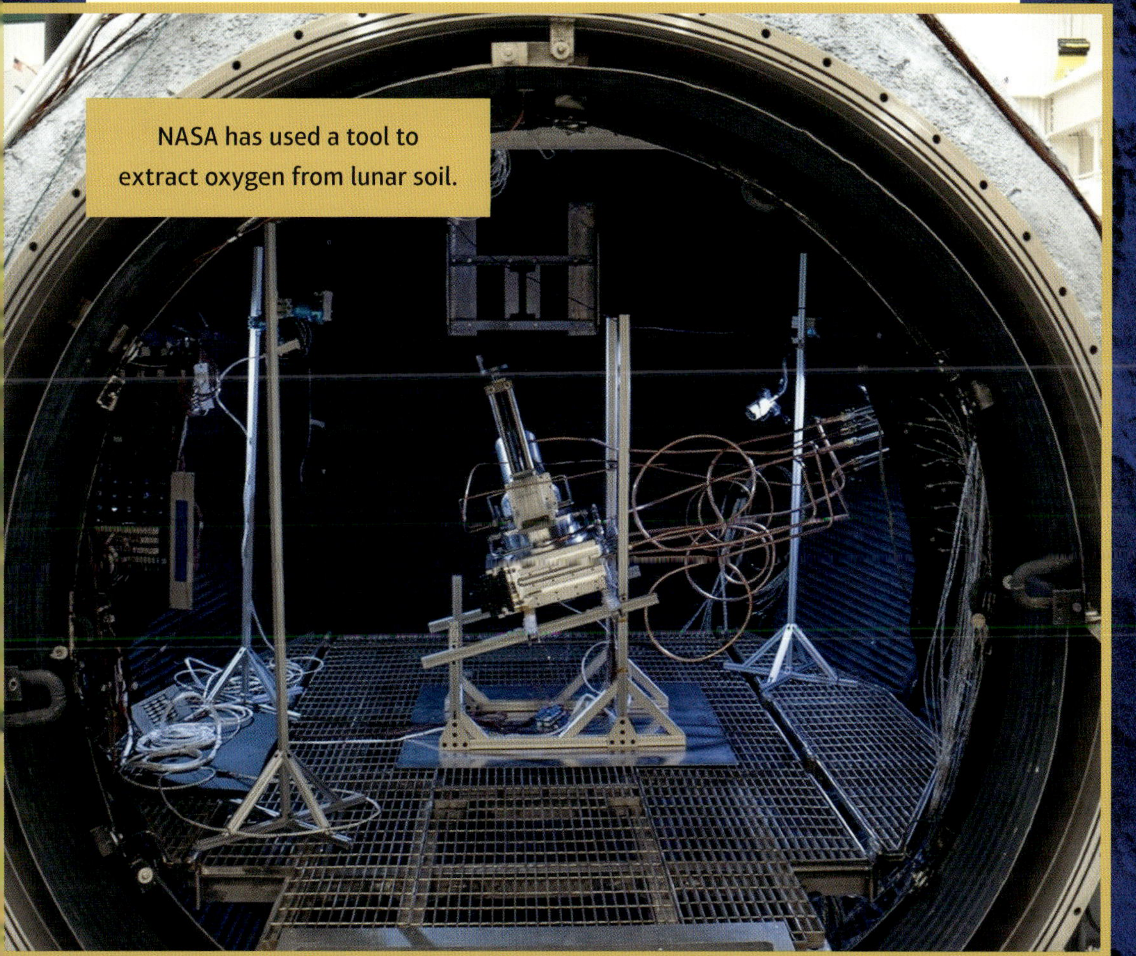

NASA has used a tool to extract oxygen from lunar soil.

DIVE INTO SPACE

Astronauts learn to walk in space by diving into NASA's Neutral Buoyancy Laboratory pool! It is one of the biggest indoor pools in the world. The underwater environment is similar to microgravity on the moon. Astronauts train to do everything on the moon from walking and wearing spacesuits to taking rovers for test drives. They even repair spacecraft and do experiments underwater.

Astronauts go underwater to practice spacewalks.

Neutral Buoyancy Laboratory (NBL) is an astronaut training facility located near the Johnson Space Center in Houston, Texas.

Moonikin "Campos" was one of three test dummies aboard the Artemis 1 mission.

CHAPTER 4

A NEW MOON WORLD

Artemis is the next big space exploration program, and it's one of the most daring ever. To make it happen, NASA is part of an international team. The team includes space agencies and private companies from Australia, Canada, Italy, Japan, Luxembourg, the United Arab Emirates, and the United Kingdom.

Artemis starts with five exciting spaceflights. Each mission builds on the ones before it to get humans closer to living on the moon.

Orion Liftoff

Orion is the mission's reusable spaceship. It is designed to carry astronauts safely to the moon and beyond into deep space—and return them to Earth. Orion launches with NASA's Space Launch System, a new heavy-lift rocket.

Orion was used to launch the Artemis 1 mission in November 2022. This was a test mission that traveled 279,617 miles (450,000 km) to orbit the moon and deep space, before returning in December. Artemis 1 did not carry humans onboard. It did carry three test dummies called Moonikins. They were used to test safety features.

The Artemis 1 flight test launched aboard the Orion spacecraft from the Kennedy Space Center in Florida.

Making Space History

Artemis 4 takes the mission to an exciting new level. Astronauts aboard Orion will deliver a core part of the Lunar Gateway. The Gateway will be like the ISS. Instead of orbiting

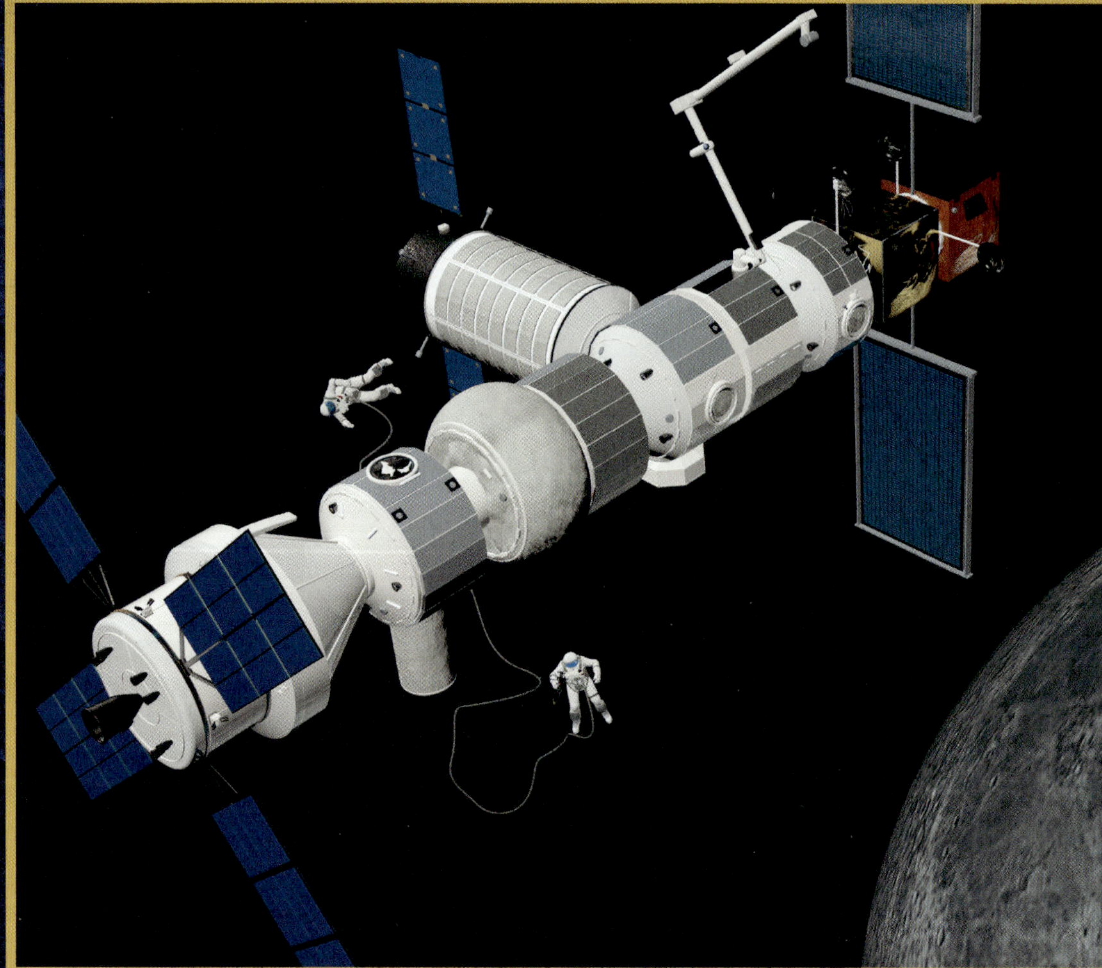

The Lunar Gateway will support deep space exploration to the moon and beyond.

Gateway Lunar Space Station

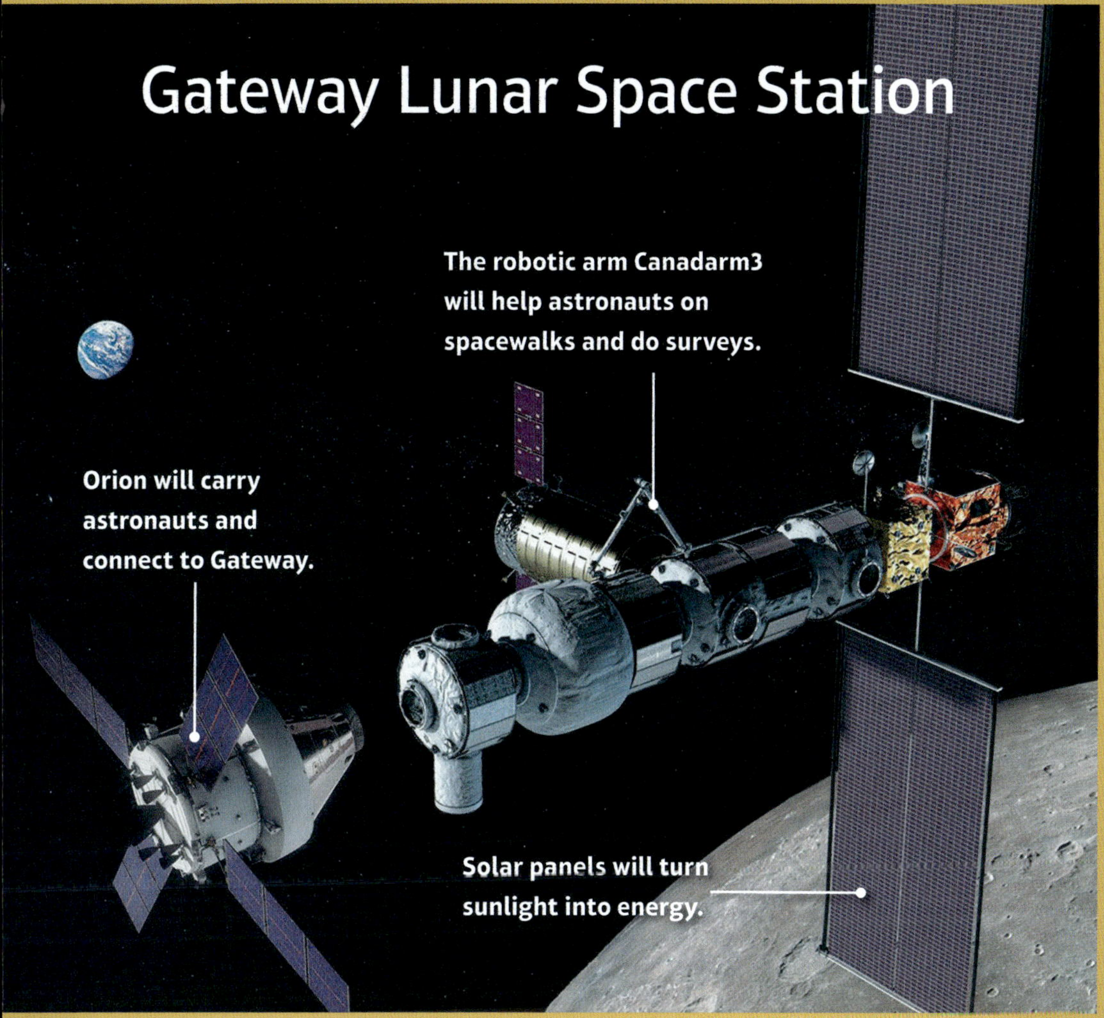

The robotic arm Canadarm3 will help astronauts on spacewalks and do surveys.

Orion will carry astronauts and connect to Gateway.

Solar panels will turn sunlight into energy.

Earth, it will orbit the moon. The Gateway will be an outpost in space where astronauts live and work while exploring the moon and deep space.

The Artemis 5 mission will carry another section of the Gateway. It will also send two astronauts to the moon's surface for exploration. NASA and its partners plan to complete the Artemis 5 mission by 2030.

SpaceX, a private company, is building the human lander to transport astronauts from the Lunar Gateway to the moon.

From the Moon to Mars

The Gateway is a first step toward living on the moon. From the Gateway, a human lander will transport astronauts and robots to the moon's surface. Early plans include making an Artemis base camp on the moon. The base camp may feature a lunar cabin, a rover, and perhaps a mobile cabin. From there, the plan is to build a lunar space colony where humans can live, work, and explore.

NASA has an even bigger mission in mind. The plan is to explore the moon to prepare to go even farther in space. The moon may someday become a rest stop on the way to Mars!

Can you imagine what a future moon colony might look like?

GLOSSARY

extract: to remove or take out

flyby: a flight that goes past a place but doesn't land there

lunar: being related to or taking place on the moon

magnetic field: the area around Earth where the magnetic force generated by the planet has an effect

microgravity: very weak gravity; gravity is the force that attracts all objects to one another

orbit: a regular, repeating path that one object in space takes around another one

radiation: a form of energy that moves outward from its source; some types of radiation can be dangerous

rover: a robot vehicle that explores planets in space

Soviet Union: a country that was once made up of Russia and 14 other republics; the nation dissolved in 1991 and separated into 15 countries: Armenia, Azerbaijan, Belarus, Estonia, Georgia, Kazakhstan, Kyrgyzstan, Latvia, Lithuania, Moldova, Russia, Tajikistan, Turkmenistan, Ukraine, and Uzbekistan

space probe: a spacecraft with no people on board that travels through space to collect information and send data back to Earth

LEARN MORE

Adelman, Beth. *The Moon's Impact on Earth*. Minneapolis: Lerner Publications, 2025.

Britannica Kids: Apollo
https://kids.britannica.com/students/article/Apollo/631766

Hand, Carol. *Living in Space*. New York: Powerkids, 2021.

Institute of Physics: The Moon Adventure
https://www.iop.org/explore-physics/moon/

ISS National Lab: Space Station Explorers
https://www.issnationallab.org/stem/

NASA: What Is the International Space Station?
https://www.nasa.gov/audience/forstudents/k-4/stories/nasa-knows/what-is-the-iss-k4.html

Reeves, Diane Lindsey. *Mining the Moon*. Minneapolis: Lerner Publications, 2025.

Rocco, John. *How We Got to the Moon: An Illustrated Guide to One of the Most Challenging, Dangerous, and Astounding Achievements in Human History*. New York: Crown Books for Young Readers, 2020.

INDEX

PHOTO ACKNOWLEDGMENTS

Photo Credits: Interior; Helen Field/Shutterstock, Interior; TB3XNW/Alamy, Interior; titoOnz/Alamy, p. 4; NASA, p. 5; Castleski/Shutterstock, p. 6; Eduard Lebiedzki/Carl Rahl/Public domain/Wikimedia Commons, p. 7; Galileo Galilei/Public domain/Wikimedia Commons, p. 8; NASA/RKK Energiya, p. 9; Digital Images Studio/Shutterstock, p. 10; NASA, p. 11; NASA, p. 12; NASA, p. 13; Dima Zel/Shutterstock, p. 14; NASA, p. 15; NASA, p. 16; Elena11/Shutterstock, p. 17; NASA/Eye of Science/Science Source Images, p. 18; NASA, p. 19; NASA/ISRO, p. 20; NASA/Robert Markowitz, p. 21; NASA/Brian Sacco, p. 22; NASA, p. 23; NASA, p. 24; NASA, p. 25; NASA/Bill Ingalls, p. 26; Robysot/Shutterstock, p. 27; NASA, p. 28; NASA/SpaceX; p. 29; 3000ad/Shutterstock.

Cover: Anna Kucherova/Dreamstime.